LOOKING FOR
Light

108 INSPIRATIONS AND INSIGHTS
FROM **MICHAEL NAGLER**
ON NONVIOLENCE

PERSON POWER
PRESS

An imprint of the Metta Center for Nonviolence

Person Power Press
Metta Center for Nonviolence

ISBN: 979-8-9911727-0-7

Library of Congress Control Number: 2024946921

The Metta Center for Nonviolence, founded in 1981, promotes the study and practice of nonviolence worldwide. Person Power Press, a project of the Metta Center for Nonviolence, publishes books on how to understand nonviolence and use it more safely and more effectively.

For more information please write to:
Metta Center for Nonviolence, Box 98, Petaluma, California, 94953
On the web at www.mettacenter.org

Edited by Stephanie Van Hook and Sophia Pechaty
Cover and page layout design by Miroslava Sobot, www.mika-art.com
Front cover photo by Patrick Fore on Unsplash

*With gratitude to the Trivedi Family
for their loving encouragement and
support in the creation of this book.*

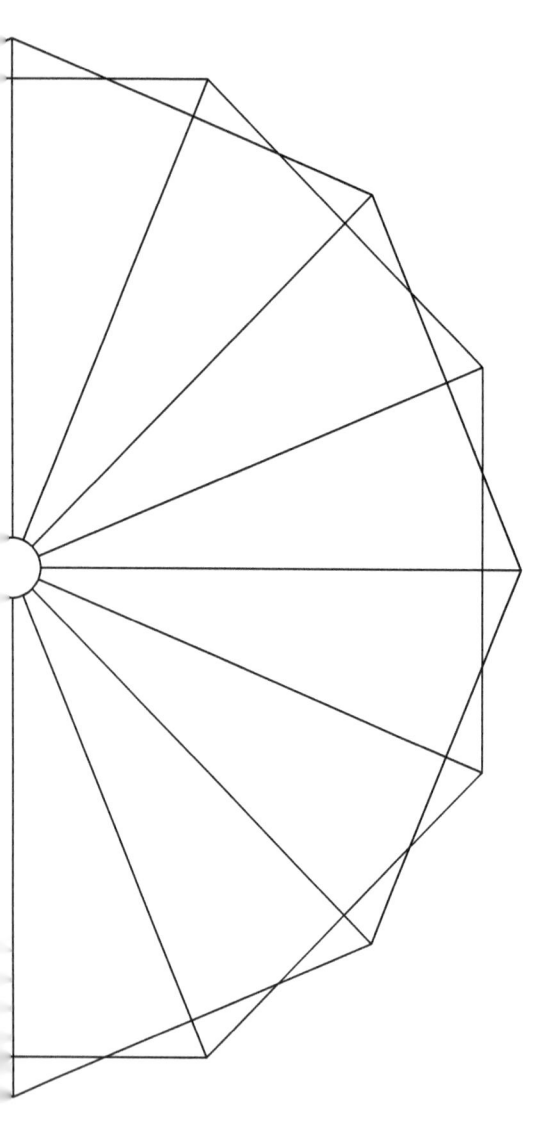

Contents

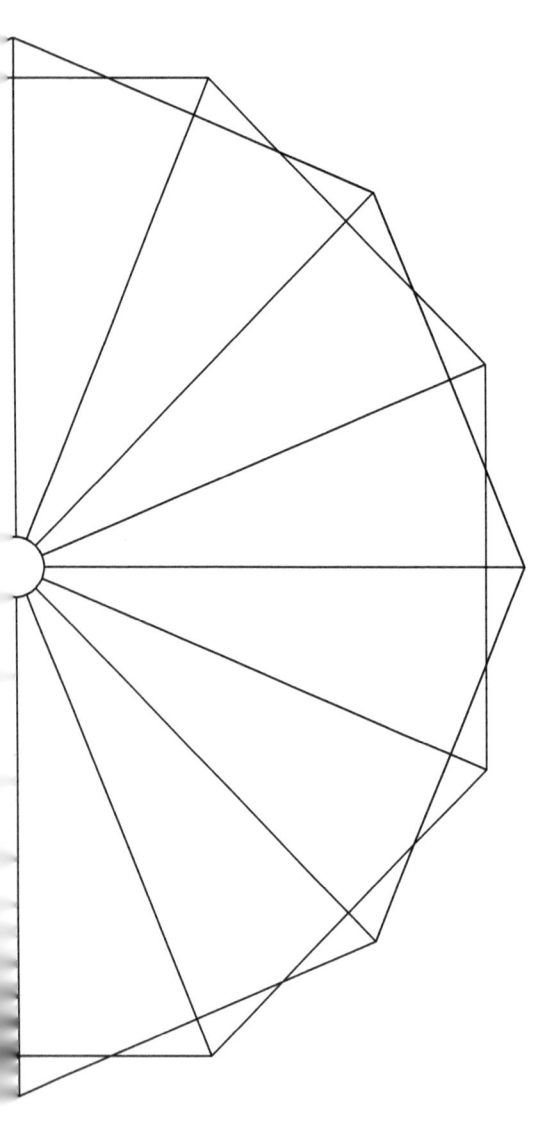

Introduction

IFIRST ENCOUNTERED MICHAEL NAGLER when I was a graduate student in Conflict Resolution, eager to explore the intersection of Gandhian nonviolence and spiritual practice. Colleagues in my field kept asking, "Have you heard of Michael Nagler?" I hadn't, so I made my way to Powell's Books and picked up *The Search for a Nonviolent Future*. As I read, I felt an immediate kinship with Michael, as though I had known him for years. His portrayal of nonviolence was rich, textured, and far more complex than I had imagined. Seeking mentorship, I reached out to him, beginning a journey that has lasted now close to two decades. Michael's dedication to spreading nonviolence has profoundly transformed my life, and I've come to realize I am far from alone. Through his teaching and guidance, he has inspired countless students and activists to rethink the meaning of nonviolence and experiment with it in their own lives as well as in large-scale movements for democracy.

Michael is not just a mentor; he is a cherished friend, and friendships forged in shared ideals are among life's greatest treasures. There have been moments when my faith in nonviolence wavered, but Michael's never does. For him, as it was for Gandhi, nonviolence is a "living faith"— not unquestioning or dogmatic, but deeply rooted in his heart and soul. I aspire to such faith.

The insights in this collection, drawn from Michael's articles, talks, and books, are meant to inspire and support all of us on our journey toward one of the greatest discoveries we can make: that nonviolence is integral to who we are. If humanity is to evolve toward peace, this realization is essential, and Michael can help to guide us on that path.

Stephanie Van Hook
Petaluma, California
2024

Stephanie Van Hook is the executive director of the Metta Center for Nonviolence.

"*Yight!*"

~Michael's first word, uttered,
prophetically, when his mother said "light"
pointing to the light that was on overhead.
(Michael himself has no memory of this
highly significant event).

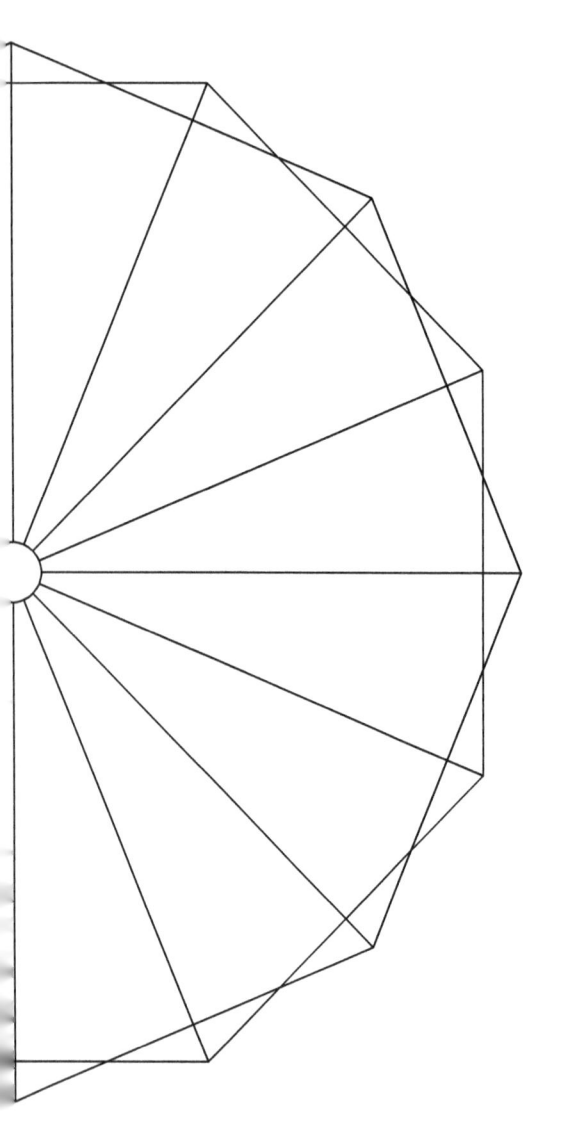

108
Inspirations
and **INSIGHTS**

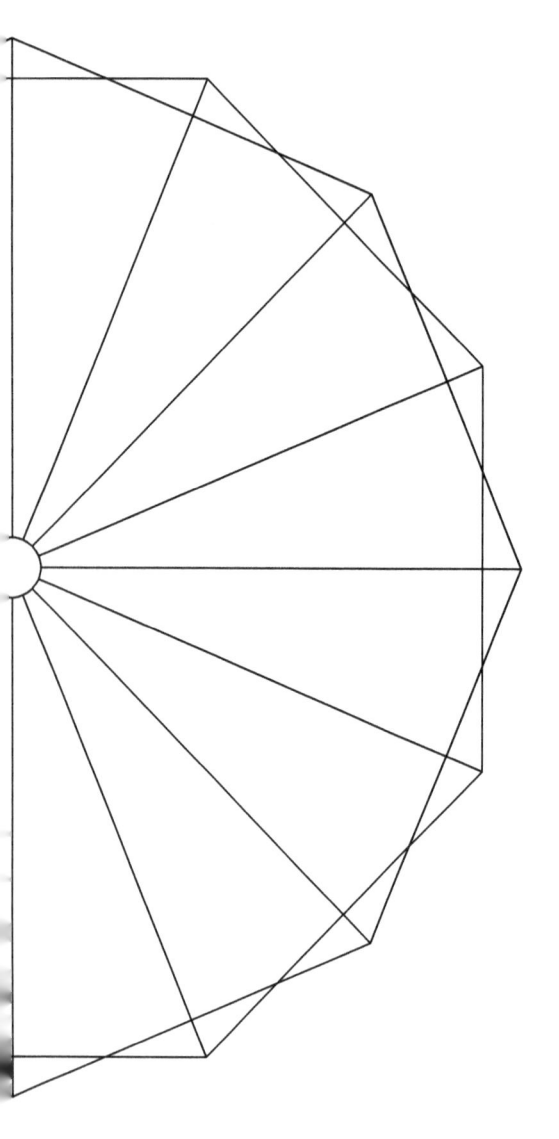

1

99

The **WORK** is not so much to *put a different kind of people in power* as is it to ***awaken a different kind of power in people***.

2

There is a **BILLBOARD** that I used to
see in Petaluma on my way to work in the
morning, trying to sell you some real estate:
'Our pain is your gain.'
What it is saying is that we are separate;
that you should actually **ENJOY 'OUR' PAIN**,
because you will be gaining something.
**Whether we know it or not, it is a very
VIOLENT MESSAGE**. It would be better,
I think, if it were obviously violent, but it is
the infrastructure for a violent world:
predisposing us to believe that we're **SEPARATE**,
and not only separate, but so **RADICALLY
SEPARATE** *that I can enjoy your pain,
or have to make you suffer in order to flourish.*

3

99

Nonviolence
is the *bridge* between
SPIRITUAL DEVELOPMENT
and **SOCIAL CHANGE**.

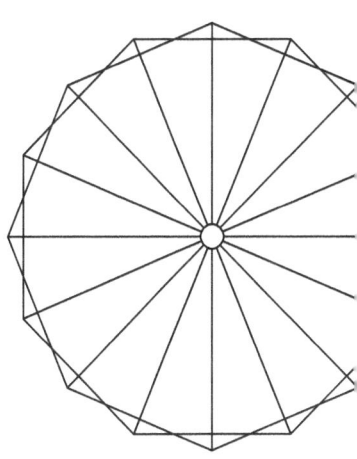

4

We are mind, body, and spirit.
What I've come to believe is that as
BODIES, we are naturally separate;
as **MINDS**, we can resonate; and as
CONSCIOUSNESS, we are one.
There are no divisions in
consciousness, and there cannot be
because consciousness, whatever it is,
does not operate in space-time.
*It's a mystery how something that exists
in space-time, our physical realities,
our bodies, can interact with something
that does not.* **BUT IT DOES.**

5

99

Gandhi made a great discovery:
that even more important than protest
and insurrection was what he called
'CONSTRUCTIVE PROGRAMME.'
With constructive program, you can
build the SYSTEMS that you want,
then the systems that you don't want will
often tend to go away, because they've
become irrelevant and they've been
superseded. *And if they don't,*
you will be in a very strong position
to make them go AWAY.

6

If there is a **spark of humanity**, even in a person who has been as violently conditioned as a Gestapo officer, that means that there is **'THAT OF GOD IN EVERY MAN,'** as the founder of the Society of Friends (Quakers) George Fox said. *Our job is to find it.*

7

"

When we're **ANGRY** about an injustice, remember two things: we are angry about an **INJUSTICE**, not at the people who are operating it; and second, we should look for *CONSTRUCTIVE WAYS* to *channel* that anger.

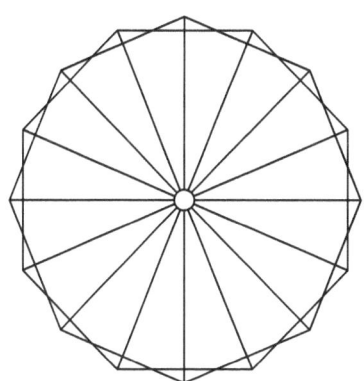

8

Take what we're seeing today under the label of **'MORAL INJURY'** and turn it on its head: ***when you are helpful to people, you experience moral healing***. It's just scientific. If we get injured when we hurt others, we benefit ourselves when we help others. And that benefit is not to be thought of as **PRIMARILY PHYSICAL**. It will have an impact on our physical being, but it's primarily a **STATE OF MIND** where we feel that we have come home. *I think that may be the best way I can put it.*

9

"

If I am *fully aware*
that you and I are
ONE,
how can I want
to *injure you*?

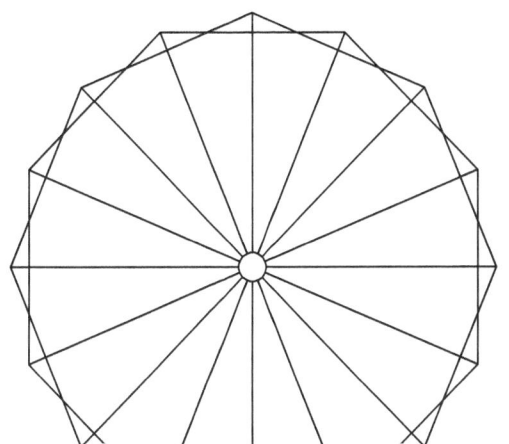

10

66

This is my faith: there is some **SPECIFIC WAY** every single human being can **MAXIMIZE** their contribution in their *own particular way*.

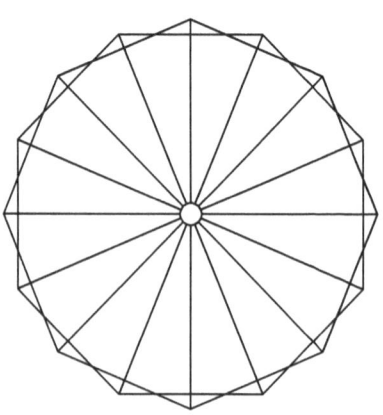

11

99

While we're doing **constructive program**, we should always be ready to explain **WHY** we're doing it. In other words, we should situate it in the context of the **NEW STORY**. Because I think that's *how human beings change* – by getting a **NEW IDEA** and seeing it in **PRACTICE**. If we just do constructive program and then go home and feel good about ourselves – even deservedly so – we are not enjoying the full potential of our actions. *We are not maximizing the impact of what we have done, which would be a pity.* To do it and then explain why we did it and how it works: **BOTH OF THESE COMPONENTS ARE ESSENTIAL**.

12

I don't think capitalism is the problem.
I think greed is the problem.
In capitalism, people who have capital employ it to create **MANUFACTURING INSTITUTIONS**, or what have you. But if you look, for example, at the Mondragón Cooperatives in northern Spain (and there are several other communities around the world), these are people who are not opposed to the accumulation of capital. But they say – and this is where Gandhi's concept of trusteeship comes in – *when you've accumulated capital, you're not supposed to hoard it.* You're not supposed to keep it out of circulation. *YOU'RE SUPPOSED TO USE IT FOR THE ECONOMIC AND OTHER BENEFITS OF HUMAN BEINGS.*

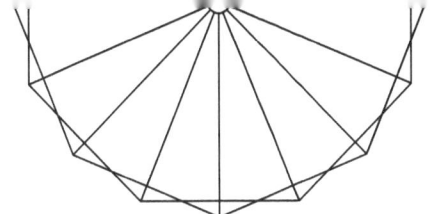

13

99

Let's not make the common mistake and say *'I picked up a protest sign and waved it in the face of that policeman, and I still don't have justice.'* This is not beginning to employ the **full power NONVIOLENCE** has to offer.

14

No. I think this is the great benefit of the scientific vision of nonviolence. We wouldn't say that a tiny little force would be enough to move a mountain. We need more. So, a tiny little bit of strategic nonviolence is not enough to make a significant impact on society. **WE NEED DEEPER, BETTER NONVIOLENCE.** *This means people have to be* **TRAINED***, have to be* **EDUCATED***, and we have to have a* **REALLY GOOD STRATEGY***.*

15

"

If you wait until a
CONFLICT has reached
its *most extreme state*,
it will require *tremendous
sacrifice* to undo that
VIOLENCE.

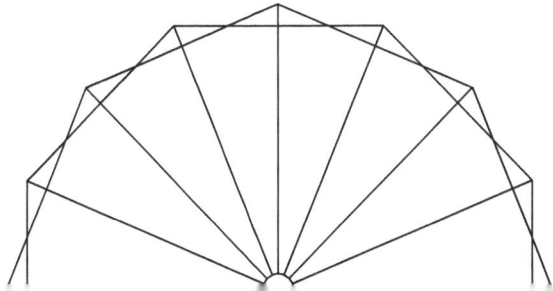

16

Gandhi was very clear that
PASSIVITY and **COWARDICE**
are forms of violence, and that
'nonviolence is the most
powerful force that humankind
has been endowed with.'
We say that at Metta all the time.
But we need to learn how to
employ it.

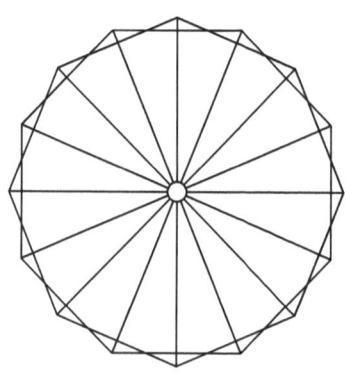

17

99

We can function ***beautifully*** in the outside world and also cultivate the **LOVE OF GOD**. *Those two things are not in contradiction – they are* ***MUTUALLY REINFORCING*** *and* ***COMPLEMENTARY***.

18

Remember, you are not against the *person*, but the **INJUSTICE** they might be doing.
The more you're aware of this – *of having no animosity against persons* – the more effectively you can **RESIST** their *behaviors*.

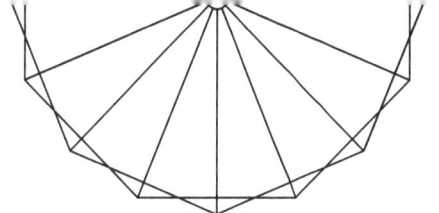

19

"

DEPENDENCY
creates the conditions
for violence. Ask yourself,
*'What are they
holding over me?'*
Renounce it.
Then you're **FREE**.

20

One of the most
difficult moments
to get right in
a nonviolent struggle
is when you've **WON**.
*By triumphing we can
lose everything.*

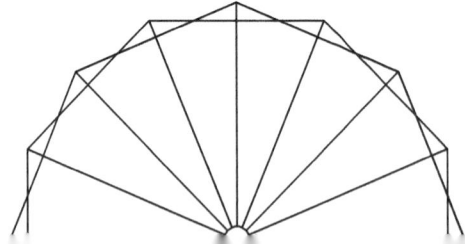

21

"

When a person is **DISTRAUGHT** or **ANGRY** with us, we have learned by practicing in our own minds to regard that anger as a **DISTRACTION**: *it is not what that person is, it is what that person is feeling at the moment.* And that enables us to make a direct appeal to the heart of that person. This in turn evokes the energy of that core and enables it to become manifest in the outer world; *that is the dynamic of nonviolence.*

22

To practice nonviolence *successfully* is pretty daunting. And I do believe that it's only **LEARNING** to control impulses that arise in the mind that makes it *possible* to do that.

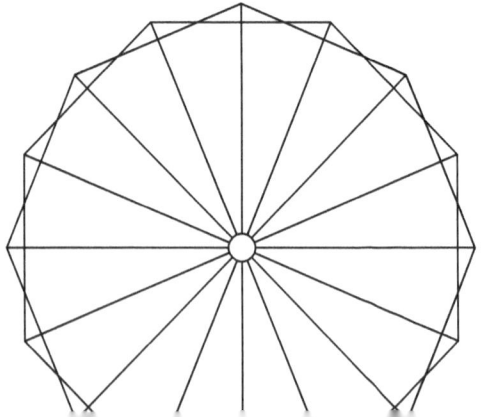

23

99

ANGER is primordially just an **energy** that wants you to act. We're *conditioned* to blurt it out in a form in which it expresses itself and we think that's being *real* and *legitimate*, but actually it's being **UNREAL** because our real self is fully at peace; **it's fully at one with others**.

24

What we're doing with a
SPIRITUAL PRACTICE
is quieting the mind so
that the **SPIRIT** can
be *liberated* and can
express itself through us.

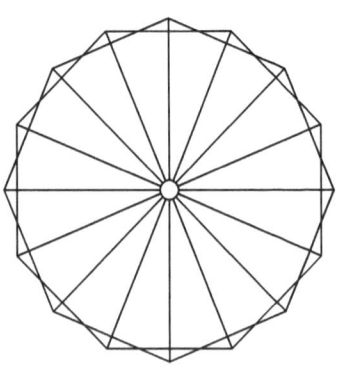

25

"

In this civilization, you are exposed to thousands of **commercial messages** every day, and if you analyze those messages, *what are they telling you*? Under the surface message, which is *'buy this kind of cigarette,'* or *'that kind of toothpaste,'* or *'put your money in this kind of bank,'* they're all telling you that you do not *have the resources within yourself to be fulfilled and happy*. This is the biggest **LIE** of corporate civilization: *happiness does not lie within us, it lies outside us, and we have to buy it.*

26

The really *powerful human being* is the one who is deeply aware of their **INTERCONNECTEDNESS** with other human beings.

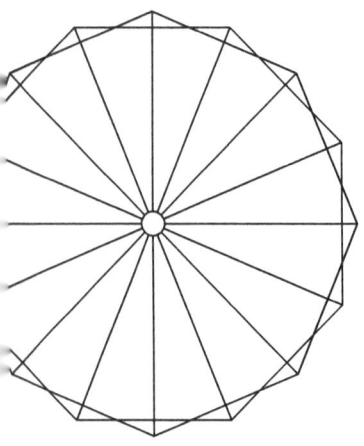

27

"

It is always better to *prioritize* working on a **CONSTRUCTIVE ALTERNATIVE** over **DIRECT CONFRONTATION** whenever that's possible. There are some things that simply cannot be allowed to go on, they've got to be addressed. But wherever possible, it's more *powerful*, and more *revolutionary* in the long run, to **BUILD** the *world that you want*, rather than **ASK** other people to stop giving you the *world that you don't want*.

28

Ultimately, the goal is not to love X number of people but to **become LOVE ITSELF**, which means that you become a **CHANNEL** for that *creative force of the universe* that has brought us into existence, and which will bring us into a **MUCH RICHER EXISTENCE** if we learn how to **cooperate** with it.

29

99

When will we realize that our **RELUCTANCE** to *kill* and *injure* is not an inconvenience, but a **PRECIOUS CAPACITY**? It is nothing less than a **GUIDE** to **how we could live a vastly more fulfilling life**.

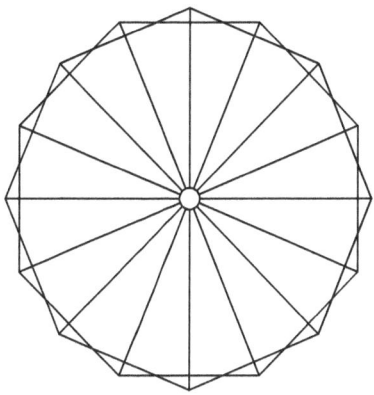

30

We are ***human beings***, after all – do we need *special reasons* to **HELP** others when we have the ***capacity*** to do so?

31

"

LIFE is sacred.
Why are we
still paying for
DEATH?

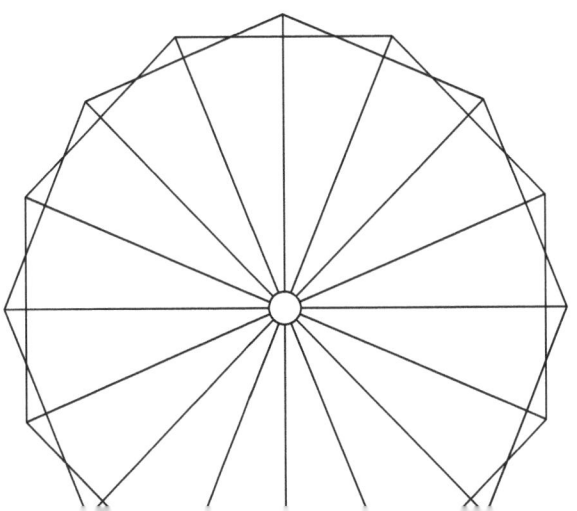

32

There is such
a thing as **MORAL
PROGRESS**.

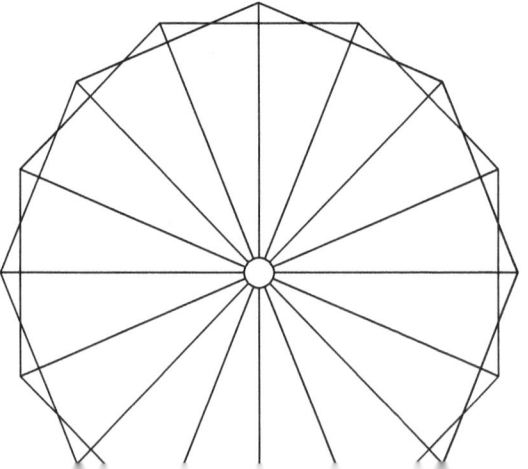

33

99

WAR is becoming an *outdated* institution. So is **SCAPEGOATING**. *The more **outdated**, the **more destructive** they become.*

34

It may be hard to predict which side will ***prevail*** in a '**nonviolent moment**,' but in nonviolence, success has more to do with **LONG-TERM CHANGE** than 'winning.' And this much is sure: *when people lay down their lives for democracy – **for all of us** – we owe it not just to them but to all of us to know their full story.*

35

"

Psychologist **RACHEL MACNAIR** developed the concept of **Perpetration-Induced Traumatic Stress (PITS)** to bring home to us the fact — now dramatically supported by neuroscientists — *that you cannot send people out to **kill** and **maim** without expecting them to **suffer enduring torments themselves**, no matter how thoroughly you try to desensitize them beforehand.* **THANK GOD!** Where would we be if this *capacity to respond to the joys and sufferings of others* could really be squelched?

36

The new sciences support insights of the **ANCIENT MYSTICS** – that we are fundamentally *interconnected*, that the diversity of cultures provides '**UNLIMITED RICHNESS**', and that each of us contains the **SEEDS** of the whole world order.

37

"

NONVIOLENCE is not meant to be a tidy compartment, the habit of an occasional activist, a musing on the margins of 'the real world.' *Nonviolence is and must become a science, a way of life, a worldview – finally, a culture.*

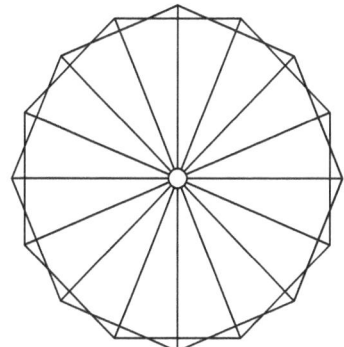

38

There are suggestive, intriguing parallels between the **universe of the new physics** and the **universe of the timeless mystics**. The deep sense of **INTERCONNECTEDNESS** and privileging of consciousness over matter supports – indirectly – *the worldview of the nonviolent*.

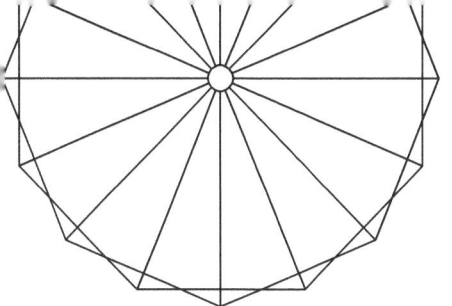

39

"

If you believe that
every *sentient being*
has its own **INVALUABLE
MEANING** and **PURPOSE**,
you cannot be a *FASCIST*.

40

"

VIOLENCE is keyed to the *lowest* image of the human being, and **NONVIOLENCE** to the most *exalted.* Violence drives us ***apart***; nonviolence appeals directly to the ***mysterious unity among all of us,*** which is the hidden glory of each of us.

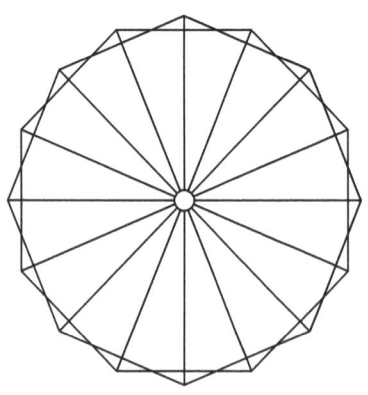

41

"

I am trying to draw a connection between a **FEELING** and a concept: between **COMPASSION** – which is really the deep wellspring of *spiritual awareness* that has held the family, society, and the planet together since the beginning of time – and the concept that all life has to be *accepted* in its diversity. I am trying to trace out the legitimate extension of **BIODIVERSITY**, which we understand, to **CULTURAL AND INDIVIDUAL DIVERSITY**, which we do not. I am trying to do this because this two-sided and apparently contradictory concept – *unity in diversity* – goes hand-in-glove with *nonviolence*. *If you will, it is the theology of compassion.*

42

"

Within the **MICROCOSM** that is each one of us are the seeds of the *whole world order*. Just as we build our bodies on a ridiculously small fraction of our DNA (and use a similarly ridiculous fraction of our brain), somehow, in the *depths of our consciousness*, each of us contains enough 'information' – faith, insight – *to regenerate a world*.

43

99

The word **COMPASSION**
means literally *suffering with
others*, feeling what they are
feeling. Of course it may hurt,
but isn't it better to suffer with
others and **EXPAND**, than
to *wall off our humanity from
them and die within?*

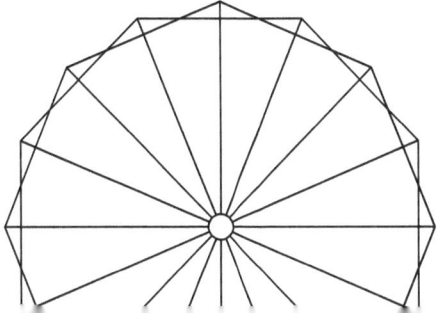

44

NONVIOLENCE is a way to *restore the capacity to*, as a student of mine said recently, '*humanize your enemy and let your 'enemy' humanize you*.' You can do this in action, where often the fact that you are being nonviolent – i.e. responding with courage and respect under duress – raises your image in the opponents' eyes. Or we can all do it culturally, by **raising the 'background' sense of humanity** that surrounds all conflicts and all relationships.

45

We need **MIND** and **HEART** together. '*Compassion,*' says the Dalai Lama, '*is the radicalism of this age.*' And I would add, *nonviolence is its science.*

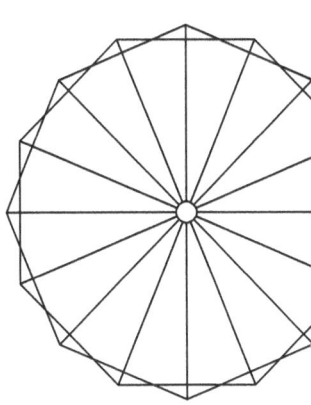

46

"

A **HUMAN BEING** — any human being — must be held worthy of redemption from *even our most grievous misdeeds*, not because we have faith in a celestial father figure who rewards the just and punishes the unjust, but *because we have faith in people*.

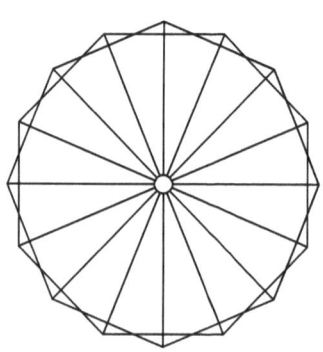

47

99

As we've been urging at the **METTA CENTER** for some time, every individual who wants to make their *maximum contribution* to the **GREAT CHANGE** we all need should stop **patronizing the mass media** that got us into this mindset of *alienation* and *greed* in the first place. They should replace that culture, with its desperately low image of the human being, with the culture — for it is one — of **NONVIOLENCE**. Read all the Gandhi you can get your hands on. We have 'moved our money;' beautiful. *But we'll be amazed what happens when we move something much more powerful than money:* **OUR MINDS**.

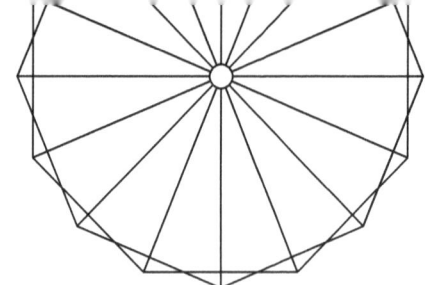

48

We are up against very serious
entrenched interests, backed
by virtually limitless money
and physical force. They can be
OVERCOME, because evil is always
vulnerable and because money
and force are limited instruments,
but we must be prepared to meet
it with an equivalent force of
COMMITMENT and **SACRIFICE**.

49

99

We will have to decide on what I call a '**KEYSTONE ISSUE**' — something that's winnable and well-aimed enough that succeeding at it will *weaken the entire violent system*.

50

We should all be conversant with the way both **MODERN SCIENCE** and the world's **SPIRITUAL TRADITIONS** agree that we are not separate, material creatures doomed to compete for scarce resources; *we are deeply interconnected with one another, all life, the planet that nourishes and houses us*. Our fulfillment comes from **RELATIONSHIPS**, not consumption; our security comes from turning enemies into **FRIENDS**, not from eliminating them.

51

99

There are two things a **DEMOCRACY** cannot *tolerate* without losing its fundamental character: **SECRECY** and **VIOLENCE**. The latter may not be as obvious, but think about it: *democracy derives its whole meaning from the sanctity of life, the worth of the individual.* ***Violence negates both.***

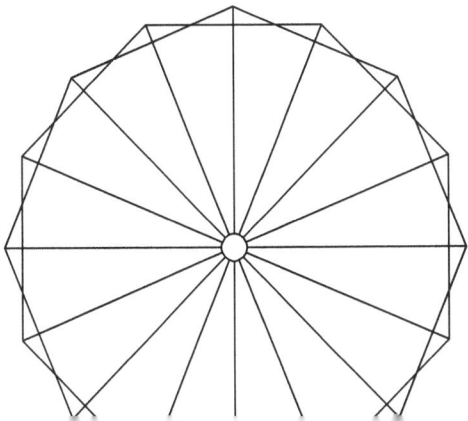

52

"

In the end, the entire system of **WAR** and **MILITARISM** will have to be replaced by **NONVIOLENT EQUIVALENTS** — and they do exist — *if we want our democracy to be real*.

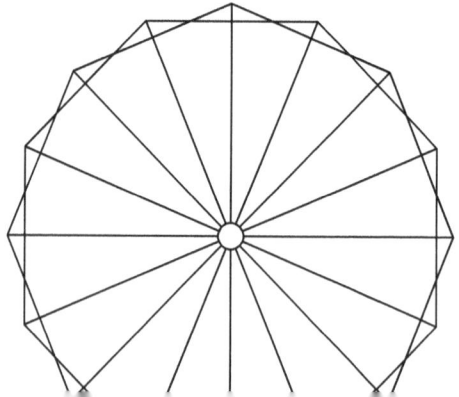

53

99

If the **PHYSICAL UNIVERSE** were not governed by laws, science would not be possible. In the same way, if there were not laws governing the **SPIRITUAL UNIVERSE** within human nature (and all nature), great mystics like **JESUS**, the **BUDDHA**, and in our own age **MAHATMA GANDHI**, would not have been able to make their *tremendous discoveries* or, if they did, *to communicate them to the rest of humanity*.

54

Because, while numbers were on the
opponents' side — along with weapons,
money, and the other accouterments
of force — *every spiritual law was
against them*; primarily the overriding
LAW OF UNITY to which all sages and
most of modern science attest, which
is the **MOTHER OF ALL SPIRITUAL
LAWS** and which we can never break,
though we stubbornly work at breaking
ourselves against it.

55

"

If we practice **SATYAGRAHA** and explain to others that it is based on principles now supported both by the best of modern science and the enduring wisdom of humanity down the ages, *we are bound, in the long run, to overcome the **dismal, dehumanizing worldview** that is causing **vast suffering** in the world.*

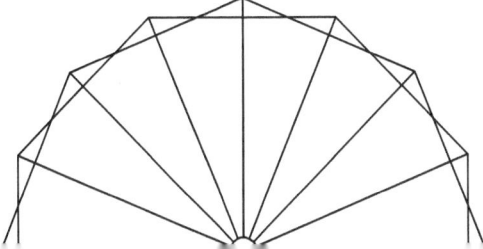

56

We can get far in this work with only **TWO FOUNDING PRINCIPLES**, which we do not need to take on faith. We can hold them as hypotheses and test them out in our own experiences: *that there are* **spiritual laws** *in the universe, and they can be discovered and used; and that despite all appearances,* ***love flows in the heart of every human being***.

57

"

That the **UNIVERSE** has a
meaning, that it is pervaded
by **SPIRITUAL FORCES**
that every one of us can use
to fulfill that meaning, is the
Good News of the Century.

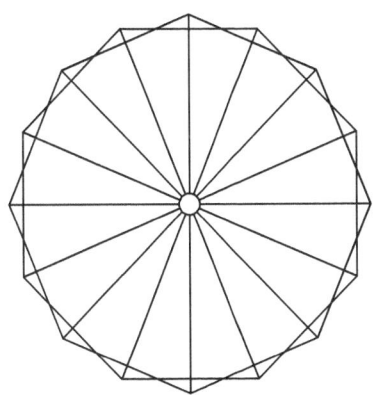

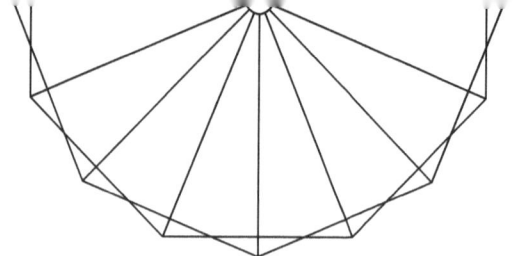

58

We have every **RESOURCE** now at our disposal to manifest the *brighter alternative of nonviolence*.

59

99

It's such an important concept, this idea of what Gandhi called a **LIVING FORCE**, meaning it's not just a neutral, physical force like gravity or electricity. The fact is that nonviolence is not just a set of actions, it's not just a moral prescription that you follow, *it is actually a force that influences minds and hearts*, and we can learn to play along with that force.

60

Where does violence come from?
I think it ultimately comes from an
instinct for **SELF-PRESERVATION**.
Where does nonviolence come from?
It also comes from the instinct
for self-preservation but with a
HIGHER SENSE OF THE SELF.
We also have an instinct for
self-sacrifice: ***for sacrificing the
smaller self in favor of the
larger self.***

61

"

INDIGNITY flows
from a sense of
SEPARATENESS;
DIGNITY the
sense of **UNITY**.

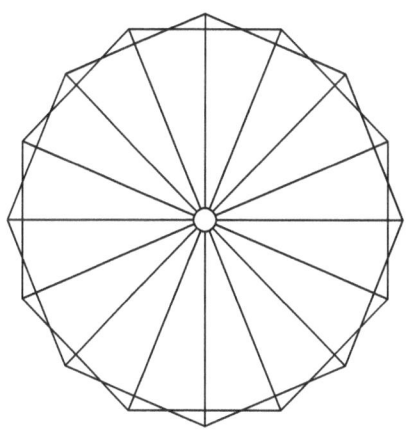

62

"

If a group has been disrespected, by raising the *dignity of that group* we raise **HUMAN DIGNITY**. That is inherently true, but I think it only really works if we do it completely ***nonviolently***, *because it is the* **nonviolence** *that really starts to sound the keynote of human dignity.*

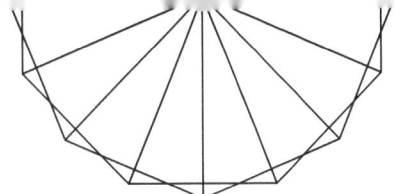

63

"

VIOLENCE affects all of us, and we don't need to be specialists to be solving the problem–*it doesn't matter if you're an activist who's spent a whole career working against an injustice or simply want to lead a more secure existence.*

64

"

Both the strength to **DEFY** and the strength to **FORGIVE** are part of a **SINGLE EMOTIONAL PACKAGE**, which makes a person capable of nonviolence. The ability to ***non-cooperate with evil*** (even at some risk to ourselves) and the ability to ***cooperate with good*** are part of the same capacity that makes us **HUMAN**, and that makes us **NONVIOLENT**.

65

"

We've taken up a belief in ourselves as **MACHINES**. But if we're machines, we have no capacity for violence or nonviolence; *we are limited in our ability to grasp what nonviolence is by **the limitations on our image of self**.*

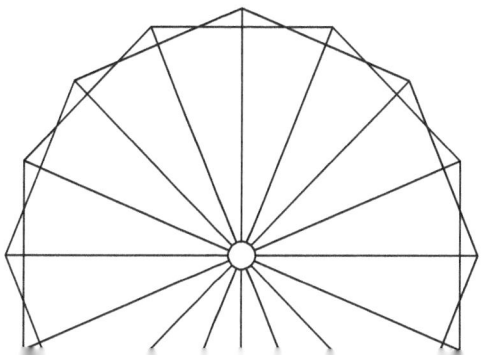

66

This is an important thing that nonviolent actors have to do: *find the* **RESIDUAL HUMANITY** *in the opponent and awaken it through their own act of* **SELF-SACRIFICE**.

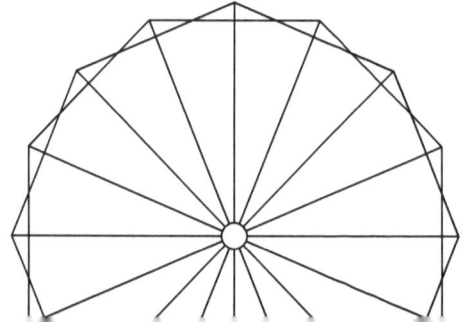

67

99

We tend to see dilemmas in terms of **FIGHT** or **FLIGHT**. *Both are traps.* Nonviolence is neither fight— *you are not reflecting suffering back on the opponent,* nor flight—*you're not complying with their unjust request.* You are not even complying with their implicit emotional demand that you fear them or get angry at them. *Creative nonviolence is beyond both.*

68

The nonviolent actor asks: *'What's the cause of the situation? What's my leverage to do something about it?'*

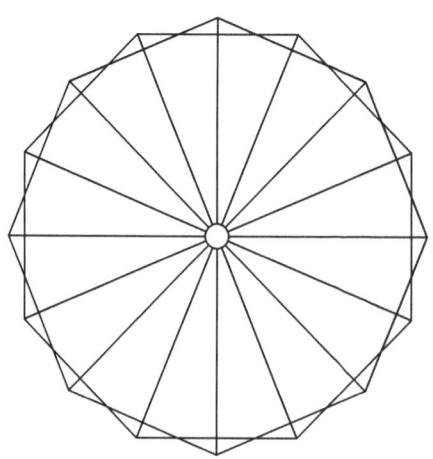

69

"

When you use violence to injure another person, you **INJURE YOURSELF**. Conversely, when you use nonviolence, to support and heal another person, you **ELEVATE YOURSELF**. You get a *higher sense of meaning*.

70

There's an interesting **PARADOX**. On the one hand, *to generate nonviolent power, you have to rise above yourself*; on the other hand, *being nonviolent means being more of yourself.* Our personal identity is never oppressed or deleted in nonviolence the way it is in violence. **DIVERSITY** is anathema to dictators, while nonviolence brings out our full personhood. We are not the **SEPARATE PERSON** that violent culture wants us to believe. **This is ubuntu:** *our real self is a self **with** others, not by itself.*

71

"

This gives another dimension to nonviolent action: *you define yourself as a different kind of person*. And I think that we now can begin to understand why nonviolent action gives a sense of meaning: *it resonates with our ultimate human destiny—to realize who are*. I am among those who believe that nonviolence is the **GOAL** toward which humankind is progressing. So when we invoke nonviolent energy and experience that state, we're actually bringing the **FUTURE TO LIFE**.

72

MORALITY is too important to be left to the *politicians*.

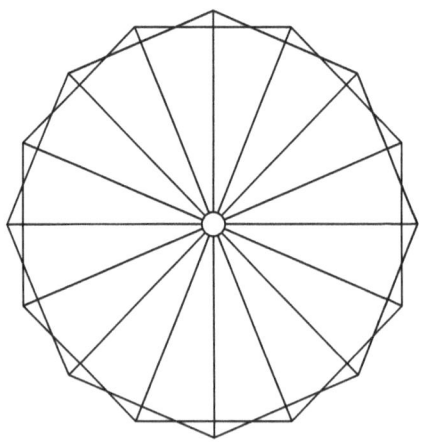

73

"

There is no **CONFLICT** that cannot be resolved in a way that *benefits* all of the parties. No good is served by *alienating parties* more than they already are. **HUMILIATION** strongly alienates people–even if it brings some *temporary satisfaction*–and reduces a potentially constructive nonviolent interaction to a *power struggle*.

74

The **UNDERLYING GOOD** of all is served when a conflict can be moved toward the ultimate goal of reconciliation. *This isn't just a **moral maxim**; it makes **solid, practical sense**.*

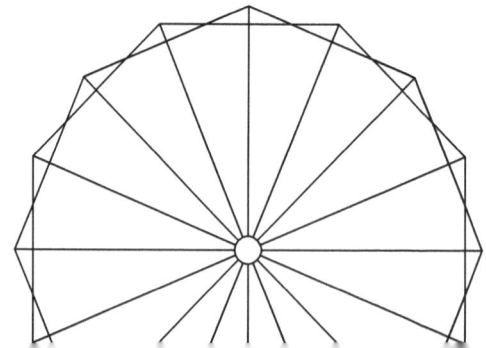

75

"

What I *urgently* recommend is when the media are drowning us in details – how many rifles, how much ammunition, what about his girlfriend – and claim they cannot find a motive—that we back up a **MOMENT** and reframe the **QUESTION**. *It isn't 'why this particular person did this particular crime in this particular way,' but* **'what is causing this epidemic of violence?'**

76

"

The time has come to say that we believe life is not for *endless consumption*, but for ever-expanding and deepening *relationships*; that life is **SACRED** (even after you're born!); that it is an **INTERCONNECTED WHOLE** such that exploiting another hurts oneself, and that security never comes from killing 'enemies' or warehousing 'criminals,' but turning former enemies into friends and rehabilitating offenders — not to mention *learning to live in such a way that does not alienate and criminalize.*

77

99

What we need to do is
close the **GAP** between
personal reconciliations
and *real policy*.

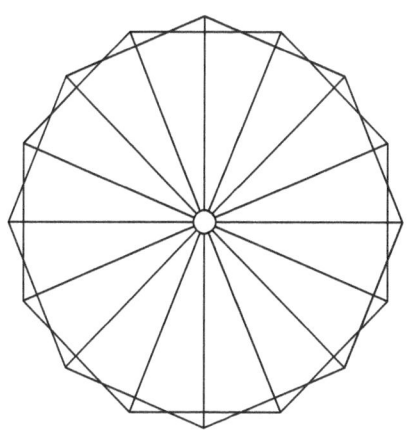

78

"

In *intense conflicts*, you can often find **NONVIOLENCE** on both sides of the struggle. *It should be seized upon, acknowledged, and supported.*

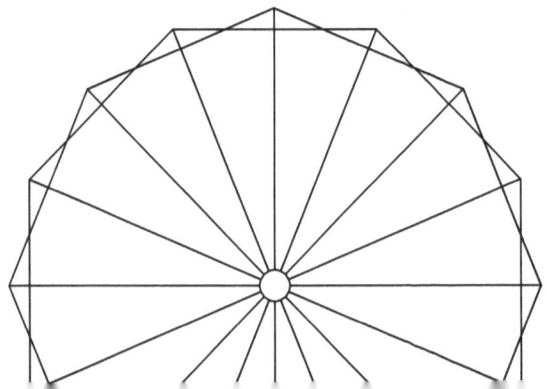

79

99

The critical aspect to real security is what's called **'COMMON SECURITY,'** where one understands that *security comes when the other is equally secure and does not feel threatened.*

80

The explosive growth of **SCIENTIFIC THOUGHT** that began in the West with the Renaissance and ultimately led to industrialism on a global scale has brought humanity many benefits but at a *mounting cost*. The problems that seem to be rising on every side can largely be traced to an increasing lack of **CLARITY** about ourselves — *who we are, why we are here, and how we are to relate to one another and the natural world.*

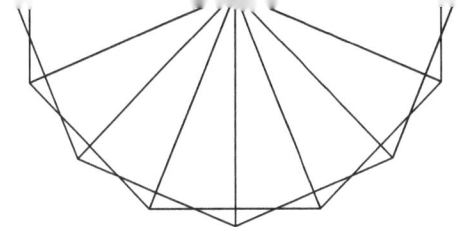

81

"

While the prevailing
industrial story is one of
ALIENATION — from one
another, nature, our own
deepest cry for meaning
and capacity — the promise
of the '**NEW STORY**' is one
of *belonging*.

82

"

While the **HUMAN BODY** may have reached an *endpoint of its evolution*, our **SOCIAL EVOLUTION**, not to mention our **MIND** and **emotions**, can and must *continue to evolve*.

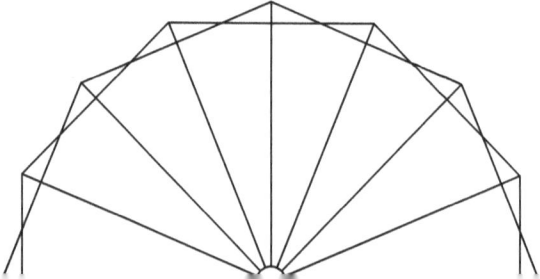

83

99

We are not ultimately
DETERMINED by our genes,
hormones, or nervous system,
but have a considerable,
often unexplored **POWER** to
determine our own destiny.

84

We can never be fulfilled by consuming **MATERIAL GOODS**; we can be fulfilled only by expanding relationships of **TRUST** and **SERVICE**. *Cooperation is far more powerful than competition.*

85

"

In this new story,
nonviolence is a **LAW OF
EXISTENCE** waiting to be
discovered and *practiced*
in every walk of life.

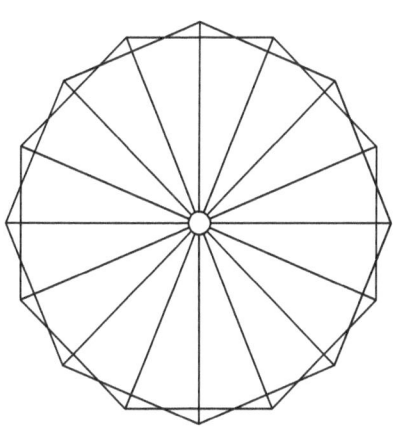

86

Gandhi understood very clearly the dynamic of the **PRESENT MOMENT**. He found by 'bitter experience' that *petitioning* should always be the first step, but often could not be the last in getting those in power to *wake up. If people failed to reach their petitioners through* **REASON***, he said, they should be ready to offer* **SATYAGRAHA** *(literally, 'clinging to truth,') or nonviolent direct action.*

87

"

No form of **NONVIOLENT RESISTANCE**, if it is to have a *positive*, *lasting* effect, can be directed against people, ***but rather against what they're doing***.

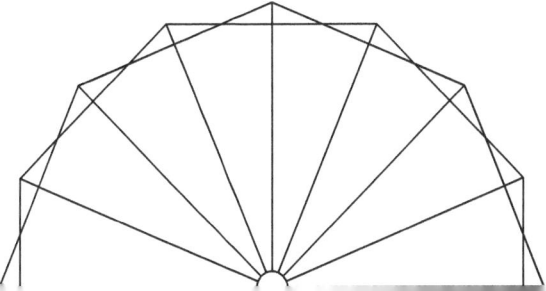

88

Let us *vow* not to stop until we have replaced the mad system of *industrialization* that's driving us to a **GLOBAL CATASTROPHE**.

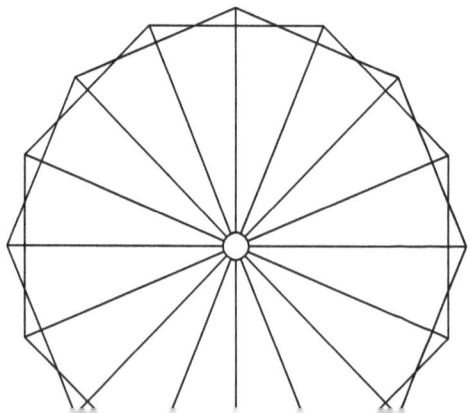

89

99

Remember that the literal meaning of **AHIMSĀ** (nonviolence) is actually '*the absence of the desire to injure*.' It is at this deep level that nonviolence makes us more **HUMAN**.

90

"

Learn *everything* you can about **NONVIOLENCE**, and act upon measures that can address the *root causes* of **VIOLENCE** in our world.

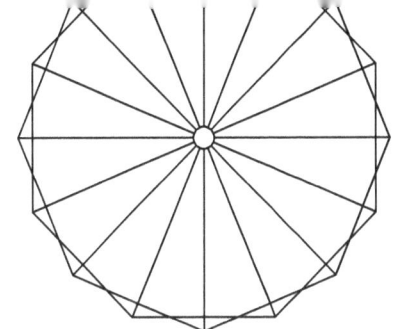

91

99

Gandhi claimed that he *'knew of no case'* in which nonviolence had **FAILED**, or could in principle possibly fail, although it was perfectly possible that ***people*** could **FAIL** to understand or use it correctly.

92

"

What happens in our own
MINDS and **HEARTS** matters;
it is the *infrastructure* of a
CURE for any situation.

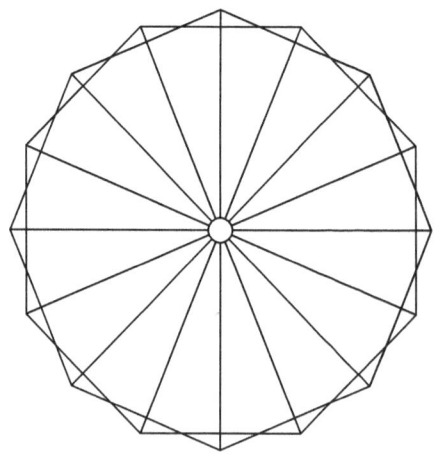

93

"

If you **BELIEVE** in nonviolence — *which implies a belief in the resilience of humanity and the meaningful order of the world* — you **CANNOT BELIEVE** that if violence doesn't work (which it does not), there is no alternative.

94

"

So far, the students say they are using nonviolence because it gives them '*the moral high ground*'. In other words, it's a **WINNING STRATEGY**. If — no, *when* — they take the next step and realize that nonviolence is the only force that **HUMANIZES** as it works, that can permanently *REVERSE* militarism and not just give it another form, I believe nothing will be able to stop them. *Perhaps this generation, with their creativity and their courage, will delegitimate violence itself.*

95

99

CONSTRUCTIVE WORK is a
powerful complement to, if not
a more effective substitute for,
PROTEST, and unwavering respect
for one's opponent (hard as that may
be to come up with) is not only the
most effective persuasion but lays
the groundwork for lasting change
because **HUMAN DIGNITY** (possibly
Gandhi's greatest discovery) *is the
basis of all justice and peace.*

96

66

In nonviolence, you try to
convert your own **ANGER**
and **FEAR** into creative,
positive forces — no small
trick — and *reject* **INJUSTICE**
decisively, without *offending*
the **DIGNITY** or **HUMANITY**
of those still caught up in its
execution.

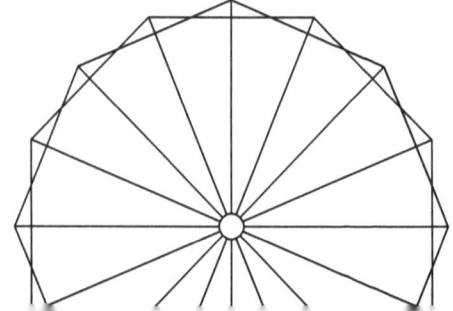

97

99

CONSTRUCTIVE PROGRAM
is what makes it possible for me
to stay *enthusiastic* in the face
of apparent setbacks, with the
understanding that we have the
practical, strategic tools to create a
different world — *one in which all of
our communities thrive, **free from
violence**, and where people can
take up, once again, the search for
meaning and fulfillment.*

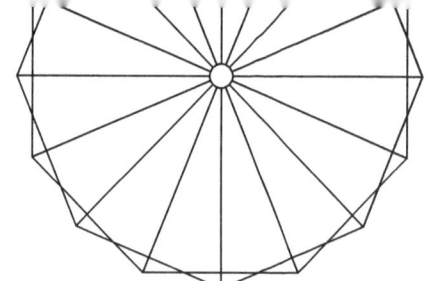

98

PATIENCE, long-term **PLANNING** and **STRATEGY**, **CONSTRUCTIVE ALTERNATIVES**, and **COMPASSION** for the opponent are much less flashy, but much more *gratifying* when you see them beginning to bear fruit.

99

"

Quite apart from its political usefulness, the new story is a **POWERFUL WAY** to overcome our own *demoralization* and *burnout*. Knowing it should be part of our toolkit, and sharing it with whoever will listen should be a **CRITICAL COMPLEMENT** of our *activism*.

100

Nonviolence is first and foremost an **ENERGY** that *resides* inside of **HUMAN BEINGS**.

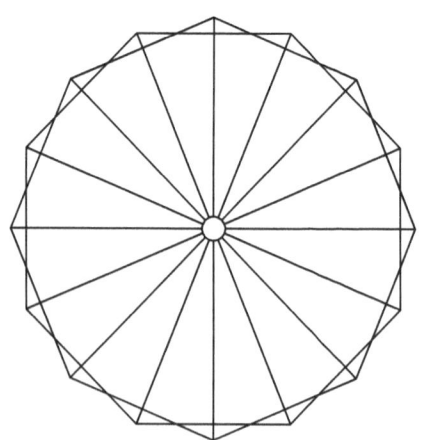

101

"

Can we live without enemies?
No. Because we have an *eternal
enemy*, which is our **EGO**. The
tragic mistake is to identify that
enemy with other people: *that
we can certainly live without.*

102

So, let's say that you are **threatening** me and I do the **NONVIOLENT CONVERSION** in my mind or my heart or wherever that goes on. And I act towards you with **respect** on the one hand but with **refusal to comply** with your unjust command on the other hand. I am now in a very **different mental state** from what you expected. **My mental state is actually being mapped in your brain.**

103

"

The question of **RENEWING A CULTURE** can sometimes be understood best by comparison with a familiar model, the *Second Law of Thermodynamics*. The prevailing culture is 'running down' toward **THERMODYNAMIC DEATH** for want of a new energy that can vitalize new patterns of order, which can help us respond to the crisis and opportunity facing us. *Nonviolence is that new kind of energy.*

104

66

There is nothing new about individuals and groups trying to **STOP WARS** by getting between groups and conflicting parties. What is new today is the **CONSCIOUS ATTEMPT** to do it *systematically*, on a *global scale*. The **GOAL** here is not only to stop this war or that war but eventually to **STOP WAR ITSELF**— *by providing a nonviolent alternative to the whole system*.

105

"

A *nonviolent interaction* is a kind of **CONVERSATION**, not a kind of fight. It's not really, or ideally, a power struggle so much as a **DEMONSTRATION** that *another kind of power* is possible.

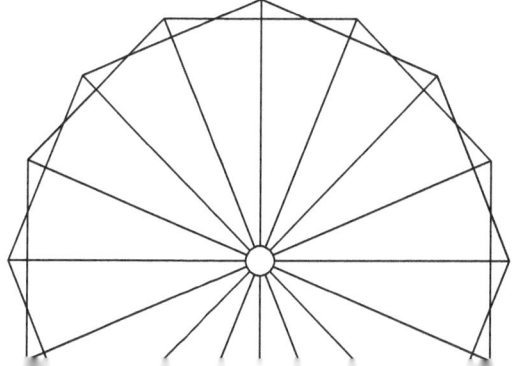

106

Every time a **NONVIOLENT SUCCESS** happens, it delivers a little *shock of recognition* that triggers the *memory* of a **LOST REALITY**, a **HIGHER DIGNITY**.

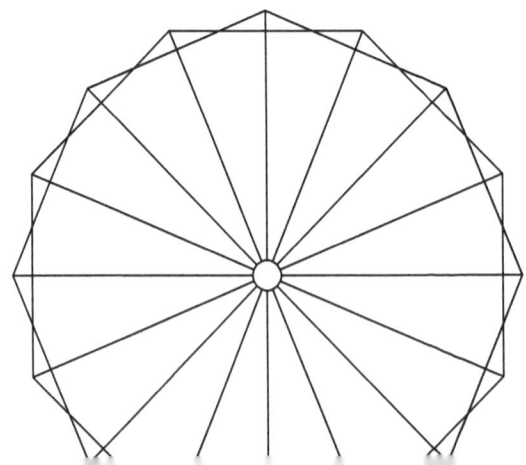

107

"

The truth that nonviolence is **LOVE-IN-ACTION** can be vigorously *creative*, especially when understood as both a **NEW VISION** and a **WAY TO GET THERE**.

108

Nonviolence is so **difficult to understand** because by nature it is what Gandhi called a '**LIVING POWER**': a kind of *unseen energy* like electromagnetic waves but subtler and much more pervasive. *It is constantly acting in living things, and we as human beings can learn to* **activate it** *in our* **CONSCIOUSNESS** *with* **highly beneficial results**.

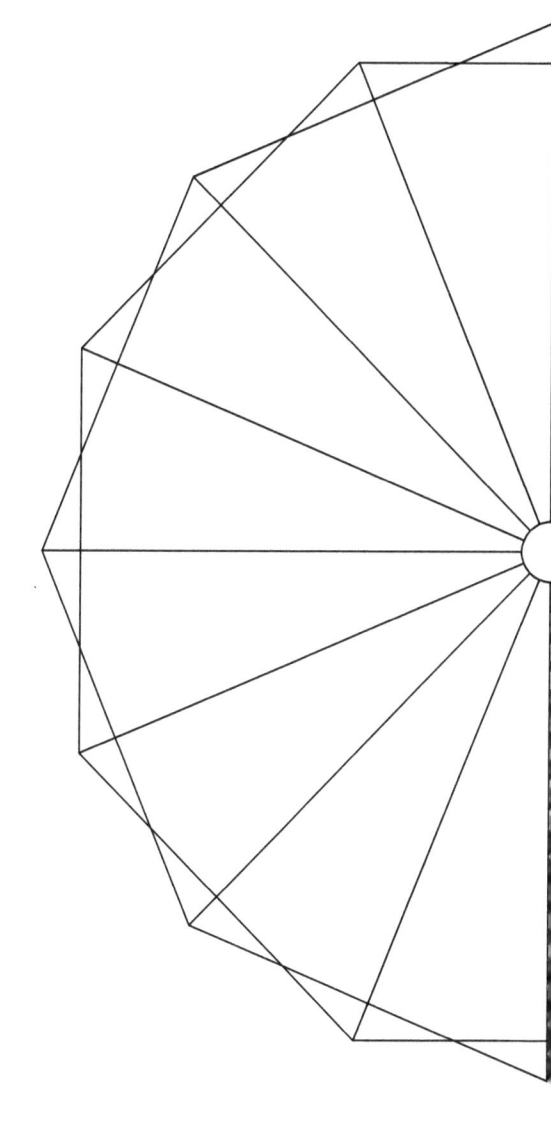

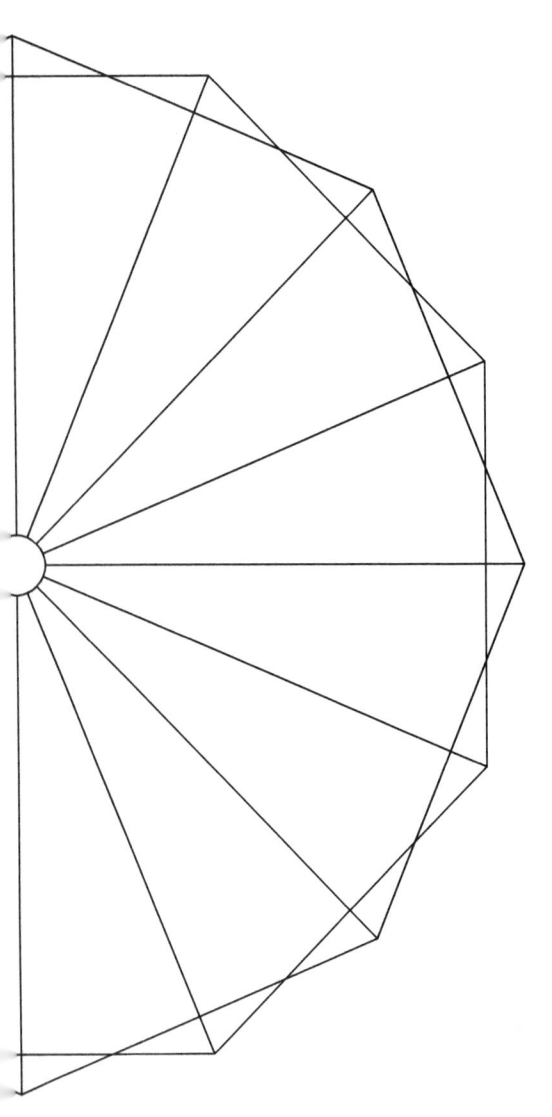

Six Principles of Nonviolence

HERE ARE SIX GUIDELINES that can help you carry out nonviolent action more safely and effectively while drawing upon nonviolent practices from your own cultural heritage. These guidelines derive, as you'll see, from two basic points to bear in mind:

We are not against other people, only what they are doing.

Means are ends in the making; nothing good can ultimately result from violence.

1. Respect everyone–including yourself.

The more we respect others, the more effectively we can persuade them to change. Never use humiliation as a tool–or accept humiliation from others, as that only degrades everyone. Remember, no one can degrade you without your permission.

Healing relationships is the real success in nonviolence, something violence can never achieve. Even in a case of extreme violence, Gandhi felt it was possible to hate the sin, not the sinner. In 1942, when

India was held down by the British and fearing a Japanese invasion, he advised his fellow compatriots:

"If we were a free country, things could be done nonviolently to prevent the Japanese from entering the country. As it is, nonviolent resistance could commence the moment the Japanese affect a landing."

He continues,

"Thus, nonviolent resisters would refuse them any help, even water. For it is no part of their duty to help anyone to steal their country. But if a Japanese person had missed their way and was dying of thirst and sought help as a human being, a nonviolent resister, who may not regard anyone as his enemy, would give water to the thirsty one. Suppose the Japanese compel resisters to give them water; the resisters must die in the act of resistance."

2. Always include constructive alternatives.

Concrete action is always more powerful than mere symbolism, especially when that action creates constructive alternatives: setting up schools, forming cottage industries, establishing farming cooperatives, devising community-friendly banking. As Buckminster Fuller said,

"You never change things by fighting the existing reality. To change something, build a new model that makes the existing model obsolete."

Gandhi initiated 18 projects that enabled Indians to take charge of their own society, making it much easier to "dismiss" British rule and lay the groundwork for their own democracy. Constructive work has many advantages:

It enables people to break their dependency on a regime by creating their own goods and services. You cannot get rid of oppressors when you depend on them for essentials. You are not just reacting to offenses but taking charge. Being proactive helps you shed passivity, fear, and helplessness.

It gives a movement continuity, as it can continue when direct resistance is not advisable.

Studies have shown that working together is the most effective way to unite people. It builds community and reassures the general public that your movement is not a danger to the social order.

Most importantly, it establishes the infrastructure that will be needed when the oppressive regime falls. Many an insurrection has succeeded in dislodging a hated regime only to find a new set of oppressors rush into the vacuum.

A good guideline to follow is: **be constructive wherever possible, and obstructive wherever necessary**.

3. Be aware of the long term.

Nonviolent action always has positive results, sometimes more than we intended. When China was passing through a severe famine in the 1950s, the US branch of the Fellowship of Reconciliation organized a mail-in campaign to get President Eisenhower to send surplus food to China. Some 35,000 Americans took part. Our message to the President was a simple inscription from Isaiah:

"If thine enemy hunger, feed him."

It seemed as if there was no response. But 25 years later, we learned that we had averted a proposal to bomb targets in Mainland China during the Korean War! At a key meeting of the Joint Chiefs of Staff, Eisenhower announced:

"Gentlemen, since 35,000 Americans want us to feed the Chinese, this is hardly the time to start bombing them."

Violence sometimes "works" in the sense that it forces a particular change, but in the long run, it leads to more misery and disorder. We do not have control over the results of our actions, but we can have control over the means we use, even our feelings and our states of mind. Here's a handy formula: Violence sometimes "works" but it never works (in making things or relationships better, for example). Nonviolence sometimes "works" and always works.

Have clear goals. Cling to essentials (like human dignity) and be clear about your principles, but be ready to change tactics or compromise on anything else. Remember, you are not in a power struggle (though the opponent may think that way): you are in a struggle for justice and human dignity. In nonviolence, you can lose all the battles but still go on to win the war!

4. Look for win-win solutions.

You are trying to rebuild relationships rather than score "victories." In a conflict, we can feel that in order for one side to win the other must lose, which is not true. Therefore, we do not seek to be winners or rise over others; we seek to learn and make things better for all.

During intense negotiations over the Montgomery, Alabama segregation laws, Martin Luther King, Jr., made an interesting observation that he notes in his book *Stride Toward Freedom: The Montgomery Story*. An attorney for the city bus company who had obstructed the African-American people's demands for desegregation revealed the real source of his objection:

"If we granted the Negroes these demands they would go about boasting of a victory that they had won over the white people; and this we will not stand for."

Reflecting on this, King advised the participants in the movement not to gloat or boast, reminding them:

"Through nonviolence we avoid the temptation of taking on the psychology of victors."

The "psychology of victors" belongs to the age-old dynamic of me-against-you, but the nonviolent person sees life as a "co-evolution" toward loving community in which all can thrive. Gloating over "victories" can actually undo hard-won gains.

5. Use power carefully.

We are conditioned, especially in the West, to think that power "grows out of the barrel of a gun." There is indeed a kind of power that comes from threats and brute force—but it is powerless if we refuse to comply with it.

There is another kind of power that comes from truth. Let us say that you have been petitioning to eliminate an injustice. Perhaps you have made your feelings known in polite but firm protest actions, yet the other party is not responding. Then you must, as Gandhi said,

"not only speak to the head but move the heart also."

We can make the injustice clear by taking upon ourselves the suffering inherent in the unjust system. This allows us to mobilize Satyagraha, or "truth force." In extreme cases, we may need to do it at the risk of our own lives, which is why it is good to be very clear about our goals. Do this with care.

History, and often our own experience, has shown that even bitter hostilities can melt with this kind of persuasion that seeks to open the eyes of the opponent, whom we do not coerce. Nonetheless, there are times when we must use forms of coercion. For example, when a dictator refuses to step down, we have to act immediately to end the vast amounts of human suffering caused by that person misusing power. Still, it requires strategic thinking and nonviolent care to do it right. But when time does allow, we use the power of patience and persuasion, of enduring rather than inflicting suffering. The changes brought about by persuasion are lasting: one who is persuaded stays persuaded, while someone who is coerced will be just waiting for a chance for revenge.

6. Claim our legacy.

Nonviolence no longer needs to occur in a vacuum; it has a long history and a compelling theory. If you are using nonviolence with courage, determination, and a clear strategy, you will more than likely succeed: win or lose, you will be playing your part in a great transformation of human relationships that our future depends on.

These six principles are founded on a belief that all life is an interconnected whole and that when we understand our real needs, we are not in competition with anyone. As Martin Luther King said,

"I can never be what I ought to be until you are what you ought to be. And you can never be what you ought to be until I am what I ought to be."

It's Not a "New" Story at All

THE EXPLOSIVE GROWTH of scientific thought that began in the West with the Renaissance and ultimately led to industrialism on a global scale has brought humanity many benefits, but at a mounting cost. The problems that seem to be rising on every side, from personal to environmental, can largely be traced to an increasing lack of clarity about ourselves—who we are, why we are here, and how we are to relate, ideally, to one another and the natural world.

The "story" that accompanies and made industrialism possible—the underlying narrative implicit in textbooks, newspapers, and films—portrays us as material entities compelled to seek satisfaction in consuming increasingly scarce resources. If this were true, competition and violence, along with the destruction of our planet's life-support system, would be inescapable. Fortunately, it is not true.

A shift in emphasis across many fields of modern science, aided by remarkable breakthroughs in physics at the start of the last century, has brought to light a far more hopeful picture of our nature, along with the inspiring possibility of a meaning and destiny that was alien to the mechanistic, reductionist view of what is now called "classical science."

In this appealing image, violence is not inherent in human nature, or in nature. Competition, alienation, and greed can, in principle, be put behind us. This vivid vision is not a new one. Nor is the image of human nature being conveyed by these new findings ultimately startling or unfamiliar.

For those who are aware of the shift, its recent reemergence has felt like recovering something precious that had, due to some kind of strange inattention, nearly slipped from our grasp.

Body, Mind, & Spirit

The essence of this new (or rather, recently recovered) story is that we can now confidently maintain that we are much more than physical bodies, despite the unvarying clamor of the mass media on this point. We are also, and in fact primarily, spirit. "Body, mind, and spirit" has been a kind of rallying cry of those welcoming the recovered vision.

For many centuries, the sages of all nations and religions have been telling us that we are not these mere bodies, marvelous as they are. Swami Ramdas, who visited the U.S. in the 1950s, gave us this inspiring picture, from the depths of his own realization, of human nature and its destiny:

On the physical plane man [sic] is but an animal. On the intellectual plane [s]he is a rational being. On the moral plane [s]he is a power for good. On the spiritual plane [s]he is a radiant being full of divine light, love, and bliss. Humanity's ascent from one plane to another is its natural movement.

Swami Ramdas' image brings us closer together and eventually to the realization of oneness: while our bodies are separate, our minds can resonate harmonically. On what we call the "spiritual plane," we are pure consciousness which is not limited in time or space.

And today we can bear witness to that vision with humanity's wisdom traditions, and with a growing section of the scientific community behind us. This is no mere academic adventure. As one writer put it, "You don't counter a myth with a pile of facts and statistics. You have to counter it with a more powerful story."

While the prevailing industrial story is one of alienation—from one another, nature, our own deepest cry for meaning and capacity—the promise of the new story is one of belonging. Despite appearances, we are passing through a time of great possibility. Yes, problems are mounting. Yes, the institutions we might have expected to deal with them seem to be paralyzed and the people at large not yet mobilized to deal with issues of this magnitude: an overheating planet, wars, and global poverty.

But the problems we face can be the occasion for a great renewal if we realize what's ultimately wrong and how we can address it. We are passing through a spiritual crisis. We've forgotten who we are and what we are meant to do here on this earth.

Happily, We Are Not Alone

People from every walk of life—scientists, artists, people of faith and so on—are already looking for a "new story" of human possibilities, beyond the narrative that has led to materialism, greed, and violence. In our search, we can hear the voices of countless ancestors who saw this truth, who lived in accordance with its wisdom and left us the legacy of their perennial vision. So when we speak of the "new" story, the story of belonging, we are really speaking of a new language to express the same truths that have sustained humanity for millennia.

What is different and extremely helpful now is how science and ancient wisdom are converging. "Science" is, in principle, a system of understanding observable patterns not only in the physical world, which is how we have understood and practiced it now for several centuries, but also in the nonmaterial world, or inner world of our own experiences. We therefore have powerful affirmation from two inquiring systems, two dimensions of science, if you will, that have seemed to be in conflict ("Do you go with 'faith' or 'reason'?"). Now these two approaches can be seen as complementary. There is an appropriate role for faith and reason in both sciences, whether we apply them to the outer world or the world within. Both are necessary. Between them they tell a compelling story:

While the human body may have reached an endpoint of its evolution, our social evolution, not to mention our mind and emotions, can still go forward. As physiologist Robert Livingston has put it, "our cognitive capacities have not begun to reach any known limitation."

We are not ultimately determined by our genes, hormones, or nervous system, but have a considerable, often unexplored, power to determine our own destiny.

Quantum physics in its way, and the science of ecology in another, tell us that we're interconnected with one another and the whole web of life. The wisdom tradition puts it more simply: "All life is one." Many—if not all—modern problems can be seen to arise from violations of this unity.

We can never be fulfilled by consuming material goods; we can be fulfilled only by expanding relationships of trust and service. Cooperation is far more powerful than competition.

We can never become secure by punishing "criminals" and defeating "enemies;" we can become secure by rehabilitating those who offend and turning enemies into friends.

In this inspiring narrative, the infinite differences among us are no longer loci of separation but manifestations of the normal diversity of life. Society, like nature, should be organized along lines of "unity in diversity" rather than those of uniformity or separation. As the Koran puts it, God has "made you into tribes and peoples so that you could discover one another," not fight against one another's welfare.

In this new story, nonviolence is a law of existence waiting to be discovered and practiced in every walk of life.

Afterword

WHILE COMPILING THESE QUOTES, I was struck by their enduring relevance. Many of them are years old; some are taken from anecdotes that have been told and retold for decades. Despite the passing of time, and ever-evolving societal circumstances, the core message of these reflections has remained urgent: that the nonviolent way of life offers the solution to humankind's most pressing crises. Michael's legacy and the work of the Metta Center sit at the overlap between the spiritually inspiring and the uncompromisingly pragmatic: a necessary balance as we dismantle our culture of violence, and replace it with a new story of humanity.

For much of our history, violence has enjoyed the luxury of promising perpetual improvement on itself. We've been taught that if only we have the biggest stick, the fastest gun, or the most destructive bomb, "our team" can "win." That promise has proven itself false. We've all but exhausted our capacity to innovate more efficient ways of killing each other. It should be abundantly clear that we are not more secure as a result.

My generation grew up practicing active shooter drills in our classrooms, learning to cower from gunfire in the same spaces we learned to read. I am too young to remember 9/11, but feel its impact seeped into our culture as residual fear, mistrust, and xenophobia. The United States has been in international conflicts for my entire life. Where is the security our culture of violence claims to have bought?

Nonviolence is often presented as naive, when in fact clinging to an outdated us-versus-them mindset is dangerously close-minded in a way we can't afford. We've followed violence to its ultimate, horrifying conclusion: we now possess the ability to eradicate life on earth. To explore a different approach at this point isn't radical; it's common sense.

The atomic bomb, the most definitively destructive force we've managed as a species, operates through fission, division, the splitting of things that are meant to be whole. At its root, this is the foundation of all violence: the underlying belief that we are isolated, separate, competitive beings. Nonviolence allows us another way forward: one where our connections to each other define and strengthen us, where our oneness is fundamental to our identity. What if we had the courage to give this new story a chance?

We would finally make use of "the most powerful force at the disposal of humankind;" a force that is active, creative, experimental, nourishing. We would finally free ourselves from cycles of harm, and replace them with a culture of interconnectedness. I hope the insights collected in this book offer you the tools to explore this new story, as they have for me.

Sophia Pechaty
New York, New York
2024

Sophia Pechaty is a program assistant at the Metta Center for Nonviolence.

About the Metta Center for Nonviolence

We encourage people in all walks of life to discover their innate capacity for nonviolence and to cultivate its power for the long-term transformation of themselves and the world, focusing on the root causes of dehumanization and ultimately all forms of violence. We aim to make the logic, history, and yet-unexplored potential of nonviolence more accessible to activists and agents of cultural change (which ultimately includes all of us), thereby empowering effective, healing, and principled action around the world.

METTA CENTER
for **NONVIOLENCE**

mettacenter.org

Your donations make our work stronger.
mettacenter.org/donate

Other books from Person Power Press:

Gandhi Searches for Truth:
A Practical Biography for Children

Nonviolence Daily:
365 Days of Inspiration from Gandhi

Remember This Always...

Excuse Me, But You're Sleeping on my House!

Courage

Find these and more books about nonviolence at:
mettacenter.org/bookstore

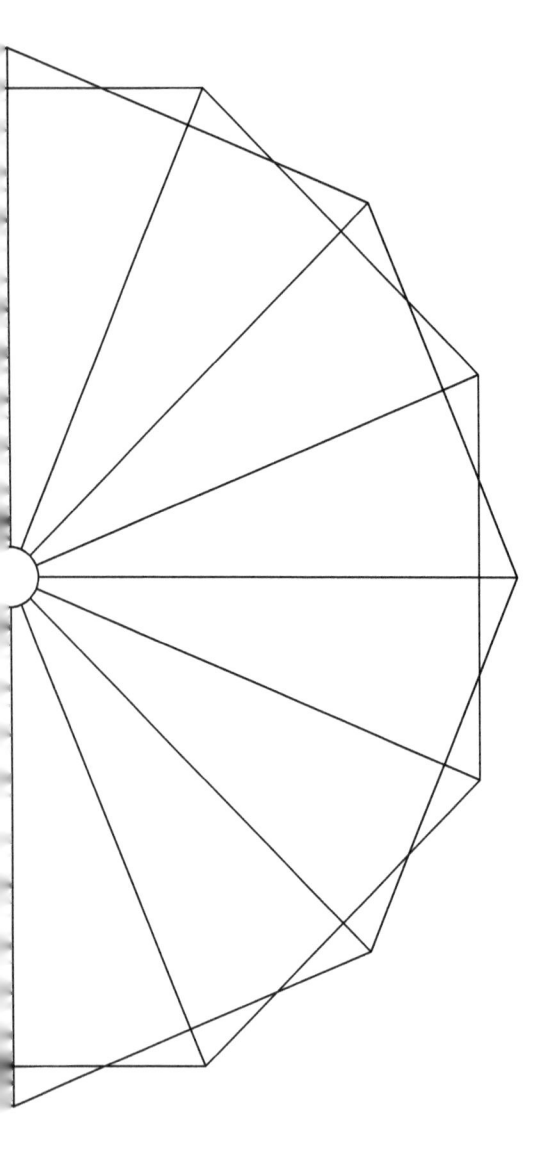